Australia July
Aug 2007

To My Darling Mum & Dad.

I thought this book would make you smile. I've bought myself the same one xxx. I thought of you both lots on our journey around Oz & always will. Jordan is blossoming before our very eyes & thats largely thanks to you ♡♡ guys!!!

All our love always
Carol, Aaron & Jordan
XXXX

Bear with me

First published in Australia in 2006 by
New Holland Publishers (Australia) Pty Ltd
Sydney • Auckland • London • Cape Town

14 Aquatic Drive Frenchs Forest NSW 2086 Australia
218 Lake Road Northcote Auckland New Zealand
86 Edgware Road London W2 2EA United Kingdom
80 McKenzie Street Cape Town 8001 South Africa

10 9 8 7 6 5 4 3 2 1
National Library of Australia Cataloguing-in-Publication Data:

Sattler, Colleen.
          Bear With Me.

          ISBN 1 74110 462 9

          1. Teddy bears - Pictorial works. I. Title.

          745.59243

Publisher: Fiona Schultz
Managing Editor: Martin Ford
Designer: Kathryn Parker
Printer: Power Printing

Bear with me

Colleen Sattler

Sometimes life bears no resemblance
to how you think it should be.

You try hard, do all the right things,
but can bearly keep your head above water.

It's easy to lose your bearings (as well as your oars),
with no rescue in sight.

Sadly, you may bear the brunt of your worries alone.

Others' beastly behaviour may make life difficult
or unbearable for you.

It might be impossible to bear your pain openly
and you have to pretend everything is fine.

The facts may be too grizzly to contemplate,
and you want to hide or run away.

Yes, many of us have some type of burden to bear.
But there is usually hope.

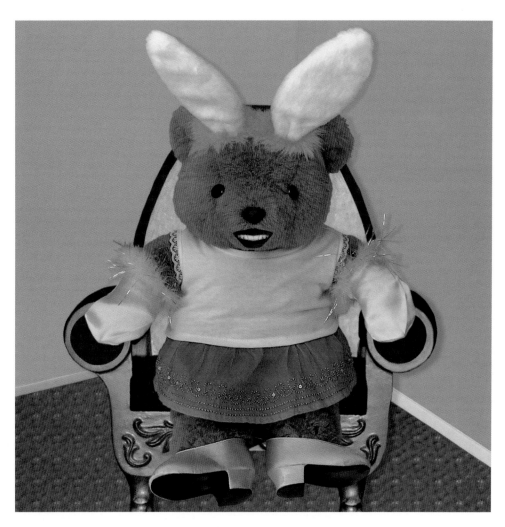

So bear your teeth, and smile a little,
even if you feel like a fake.

In a world of steel and concrete,
take a walk in the bush to regain your bearings.

Paws for a while to appreciate the
splendour and beauty of nature.

In times of unbearable stress,
lie low for a while and enjoy the sun.

If your troubles are hard to bear,
take it easy with foot-tapping music.

Or meditate. Find the inner strength to bear
any disappointment or loss.

When nothing else helps, indulge a little.
Purchase more than the bear essentials.

Though, as you know—a warm, tender bear hug
is usually what we need.

When life knocks the stuffing out of you,
it's soothing to have a good cry.

Even if it's while watching an unbearably sad movie.

At the end of a tough day,
throw off your tight clothes and wear a teeny teddy.

In times of stress and pandemonium,
hang out at home and pamper one another.

Relax and unwind. Spend the bearest—or longest—time soaking in a warm tub.

However, if you are like a bear with a sore head,
go out and rage. Party the night away.

25

Then come home, escape your daily bear pit of obligations,
and dream sweetly all night long.

If you are tired of panda-ing to others,
find a secret place to escape to.

And should you crave soothing company,
or a good listener, don't forget your teddy bear.

Occasionally you might want to beat the stuffing out of someone, but find a peaceful solution.

When you can't keep your paws to yourself,
put them to creative use.

To avoid feeling grizzly,
take up a sport or hobby and make it your passion.

For example: enjoy the magic of dancing.
It will bear you away to another world.

Read extensively to escape and understand.
The gathering of knowledge can only bear you fruit.

Dare to be your wild, adventurous self.
Even if others think you are bearly respectable.

Introduce a little excitement in your life,
ride bear back though the woods.

Travel to unique locations and bring to bear
an appreciation of other cultures and people.

Though if money is a problem and your clothes are thread bear,
enjoy the simple, free things in life.

Relish every sensual pleasure.
Walk bear foot though the moist morning grass.

Stop and "smell the roses". Live in the present moment
and you bear a good chance of being happy.

Bear a hand to those who need assistance. Helping others can take the focus from your own anxieties.

Go bearing gifts to someone who is sad or lonely.
It will warm your heart and theirs.

Bear a little romance in your life. True love
can greatly enhance your happiness and wellbeing.

Though finding the right partner can be a huge bugbear,
and a long, slow process.

Sometimes you have to strip your pride bear
and go after what you want.

However, if you cannot bear to be alone,
learn to like your own company.

Many say the greatest joy is to bear and rear children.

That caring for one's cubs is full of
life's special moments.

It's well known, a mother's love bears all things,
including sleepless nights.

And indeed, a father is the bearer of great strength,
and loving kindness.

There's much in life to celebrate. Cook a scrumptious meal for family and friends to show the love you bear them.

Know the bear facts. Eating chocolate releases endorphins
and provides immediate pleasure.

Though, when you can't bear to live without something,
you may have a serious addiction.

If you are desperate for a delicious treat,
the secret is to stop before you're over stuffed.

And when your cupboard is bear,
it's wise to fill it with nutritious fruit and vegetables.

Should your stuffing start to sag and bulge,
it's time for drastic measures.

When you don't want to be seen bearing arms
(or anything else), get your body moving.

Exercise! Bearing light weights strengthens you
and makes your skin hang a little better.

Or do yoga and bear witness
to the benefits of increased flexibility and energy.

Learn to be comfortable in your own skin,
it's the only one you are going to have.

Though of course, if you've got it, flaunt it and bear it all,
Enjoy what nature has given you.

If the desire for change comes bearing down upon you, sometimes all it takes is a hair style overhaul.

Or, improve your sense of bearing in the world.
Look your best, even on an ordinary outing.

You may never be unbearably beautiful,
but make the most of what you have.

Then accept what you cannot change. Some characteristics come from the genes of your forebears.

Only some are born with the looks of a super model.
Most of us have to bear with life's little inequalities.

And another unfortunate fact—your chores won't magically get done. Usually you have to tackle them bear handed.

And often you need to practice patience
before you can bring to bear your deepest desires.

If you feel bearly qualified or inexperienced,
the answer is to practice, practice, practice.

Bear in mind also, that sometimes
you need to strain towards your goals.

Though you can seek advice, and then daydream
that your good fortune will to bear out as true.

But when you bearly know what to do or where to start,
sometimes it's best to dive right in.

Then if things go wrong, you take a spill
and your bear bottom is on display, have a little laugh.

We all bear scars from falls and scrapes.
Often it's necessary to get up and start all over again.

When your ball bearings (and your determination) grind to a halt, a push in the right direction could be all you need.

Indeed, even when you think you are
bearly making any progress, keep aiming high.

But, while you are pawing your way to the top,
don't forget to keep in touch with family and friends.

Know that when you cannot bear to leave your responsibilities,
or your desk, it's time to take a break.

And should you achieve great success, don't look down your snout,
even friends will avoid you.

If at times you are a little overbearing,
step back and give others their space.

Try not to wake up growling in the morning.
It makes life unpleasant for your loved ones.

Speaking to others in bear-like-grunts
is not communication.

It's true, a bear-faced lie can save your skin momentarily,
but it makes others wary of you.

The truth laid bear, no matter how difficult to hear or say, will give you peace of mind.

Though respect others' privacy.
Don't stick your snout where it doesn't belong.

And if your suspicions bear out to be true,
resist the temptation to say "I told you so".

Sometimes (just sometimes) you might imagine
you are smarter than the average bear,
but there is always something new to discover.

Don't be quick to pooh-pooh others' ideas.
Listen and you may learn something extraordinary.

If someone takes a bite out of you or insults you,
often it's best to just grin and bear it.

And if others gossip about you,
be reassured that they may bearly know you.

Be forbearing of others, overlook their faults
and hopefully they'll do the same for you.

Avoid bearing grudges against your family or friends.
They are more precious than anything money or power can buy.

When your friends are feeling down or lonely,
reach out a paw and show you care.

Panda lovingly to those who are important in your life.
They usually deserve it.

And if you have been bearish, be brave and ask for forgiveness. It can save you from polar conditions.

It's comforting to find others with whom you can bear it all,
who accept you just the way you are.

But before you bear your soul to another, or make them your best friend, make sure they are worthy of your trust.

Who you bear company with can influence your life's direction. Good companions take you to their level, bad companions can too.

In fact, the case for evaluating everything in your life bears close investigation.

Your attitudes and thought patterns
have a direct bearing on how your life pans out.

You might think you bear a charmed life.
However, one day there will be an ending.

But despite any faults and failures, congratulate yourself.
It's your inner stuffing that's helped you gain every success.

And remember, don't sit home and hibernate.
Get out there and enjoy everything life can offer.

You are the bearer of your own destiny.
Listen to your heart and follow your dreams.

About the author
Colleen Sattler is a freelance technical writer, editor, web designer and copywriter as well as a passionate photographer. She and her growing collection of bears live in Sydney, Australia.

Acknowledgements and bear hugs
A huge bear hug to Peter Simpson for his loving patience and perceptive advice. Another bear hug to Sarah Napthali for her steadfast belief that one day (like herself) I would have a book published. Heartfelt thanks also to Mira Sonik, Avril Cooke, Sarah Herlihy, Stephanie Chambers, Gillian Hawkins and Camille de Jorge for their support. Grateful thanks to Joyce Kornblatt and the other wonderful women (especially Margie Sullivan) from the Seasons of Our Lives writing group, without whose encouragement I might not have persisted. A large bouquet to Julian Rego for the ingenious Photoshop lesson and also to Ginny Stubbs and to Philip Johnson (for lending me lots of photographic magazines). Much appreciation to Mary Wright for the polar bear and to Natasha Wright for the fuzzy brown bear. Warm bear hugs to the fabulous women in the Blue Mountains reading group whose spirited discussions I have missed while working on this book.

Lavish thanks to Selwa Anthony and Fiona Schultz for their enthusiasm for my book. Thank you also to Martin Ford and his creative team at New Holland Publishers.

For their generosity in allowing me to photograph their beautifully designed and decorated homes, an extra special thanks to Masterton Homes. I am also grateful to the following people for permitting me to take photos: Fiona and Michael Djatschenko from Kookawood (holiday cottage extraordinaire), Intarsia Homeware, Fruities, Bay Convenience Store, Vanessa and Julian Rego, Betty Sattler, Mark Sattler (lovingly restored motorbike), Karynne Courts (Bailey the dog), Stuart Miles (Tilly the horse), Stan Garner (Honda mower), Rhoda Case and Lara Grinevitch.

Occasionally I have changed a location in Photoshop (eg removed roof tops, windows, walls) to create a simpler background. I've also accentuated or changed the colours of some items to make the bears stand out on a page. It has not been my intention to offend anyone, the original items are perfect in every way.

Lastly, many thanks to the numerous teddy bear manufacturers for producing our cuddly friends. Thank you also to the creators of all the gorgeous outfits I was able to procure.